After Midnight

After Midnight

For those that made me feel

My Mellow,
You give me life!

After Midnight

There is the sound of the first cry of a new-born baby who is destined to make their mark.

Vulnerable and innocent, the baby will see only shadows of black and white and will trust the arms that hold them. They will grow familiar with scents and voices and these will guide them to the colours that their eyes will eventually see.

The baby will instinctively love with their whole being and will grow ready to reach out into their world.

They will see the joy of the rainbows and the shimmer of life in puddles after the rain clouds clear. Clumsy fingers teasing flower petals and tiny lungs spent from wishing on dandelions.

Gazing at horizons, imagining the more that awaits them.

But the rules of the world will come.

Programming has begun.

The little girl smiles demurely into the mirror, practicing with her mother's make-up and dressing in her heels, keeping busy so as to ignore the pangs of hunger.

Colours fade back to the black and white shadows of infancy and there is no life shimmering in rainwater.

All are shaped to the moulds of those that came before them.

Must. Not. Break. The. Rules.

But those that don the uniform of conformity are not all convinced of the norms they are told they must follow.

They march to the beat of the rule; outwardly obedient, inwardly negotiating their own way.

The revolt will start small. Quiet hushed voices in corners whispering their truths.

It will stem from tiny acts. Supportive arms around brave shoulders.

The march will stumble....

And resume...

But the mould will already have been cracked... A tiny crack leading to curiosity about all the whys behind the rules.

Questions colouring in the black and white.

Answers in the aftermath of the rain.

The march will stall…

And the long-forgotten childhood dreams and freedoms will come forth.

Their magic will free from the norm.

You slapped me
You called me a bitch

I was 12

You know those boxes of free kittens
That we sometimes see in movies?
Where people look in and decide
Which kitten is the cutest,
Which kitten is the smartest,
Which kitten is the runt?
The kittens' hopes of rescue
Grow with each stroke from a stranger
And they paw at the walls of their cardboard prison;
Their wide eyes screaming "Pick me, pick me".

You slapped me
You called me a bitch

I was 12

It'll be a bit of fun
They said

Not realising that
I've played those games before

I'm on their team
Until they win

And I
Inevitably lose

I miss you

You said

As you turned to
Another curve

Remember that time you told me that
I "got hot"?

Oh honey, I was always hot
But you only noticed me
When my light dimmed
And I faded into what
The world said I should be.

I gave so very many minutes
And now it's time
To take back my hours

Eyes wet with
Unfinished tears,
Hands furled with
The frustrations of penance.

I'll do
And
Do
And Do
Until
I can't
Do
Anymore.

There will be no freefall
From the bridge.

Smiling
At the
Out of the way
You took
To be there

So we sit together at sunset,
Waiting until it's safe to speak.

You have your drink,
I have mine.

Your gaze is fixed on…
Well…
On anything that's not me
I steal glances at you over the rim of my glass
As I take sips of courage.

You're not really here
But still I stay.

When the sound of footsteps has faded,
You dip your head,
Cup my face in your hands,
And finally your eyes find mine.

Your eyes read me,
All of my unsaid stories.

My breath catches.

You kiss me
And I am alive again.

Moving in the darkness,
I believe the white lies your lips tell my skin,
I believe in the beautiful fictions of your touch.

Your body… It lies so well.

And after midnight,
I tell you my happy secrets,
Make you laugh,
And you hold me tight until you drift off to sleep.

When your breath is even,
I will speak my darkness,
Tell you of my pain.

Let you in as I slowly pull away.

For the briefest of moments
We were real
And I could dream
Of a future that will never be.

The sun rises
And so do I.

I know you're awake but you don't look up.
Without the shadows,
I am nothing.

I walk out the door,
Held together by
Little white lies of lust and
The honesty of midnight whispers.

When the sun shone
I asked her to smile.

It was beaming and radiant
And worth the wait.

The shadows grew less,
Drew back in defeat.

Warm curves of joy,
A job well done.

She'll smile today,
In spite of yesterday's tears
And tomorrow's fears.

I'll be whatever
You want me to be
Until I'm too tired
To dance that way.

Pop a pill.
Be fine.

Pop three.
Feel like me.

The touch of
The tuck behind the ear.
The inhale of
Locked eyes and
Fingertips on bare shoulders.

Lips planting hope at the
Nape of the neck.

Daring to dream.

Each kiss the promise of tomorrow,
Each heated breath obscuring yesterday.

Foolish run.
Fearful walk.
But those that want…
Fall.

There are no resolutions
In mocking smiles

I didn't want what
I deserved
For taking shortcuts

Wandering through the nightmare realm
With only pale moonlight for a friend
I am lost amongst the shadows.

I grasp at hard stones
As I try to make my way.
There's no rhyme or reason
To their map
And yet I willingly follow their path.

All is silent
Save my own
Beats and breaths.

Until a rattling fills the air
And the echoes of mayhem are unleashed.

I wrap my arms around myself,
Screw my eyes shut.
What I can't see won't hurt me.

The earth pulls apart beneath my feet.
Iron screeches as it's bent into unfamiliar shapes.
Panicked caws from daytime birds ring through the
air.
The orchestra of this night wreaks its devastation.

Building.
And building.

And building.

Until it stops as suddenly as it started.

A blanket of hush falls
Drowning, quenching out the madness
Until all there is
Is the sound of
The flutter of the final wings
Making their escape.

I wait.

I feel the breeze.

I gather my jumbled thoughts.

I open my eyes
And face my friend, the moon.

It's brighter.
It's clearer.
It unmasks all of this night-time's secrets.

My being adjusts to the chaos.

The plots of finished stories lay open.
Each sleeper unveiled.

Cracked wood
And decaying smiles.
Their macabre peace
Laid bare for all to see.

I can't stop my eyes from drinking...
Until they fall upon the familiar.
Yet unfamiliar.

Memories of warmth and laughter
Sullied, soured by the present
Which lays before me.

The chaos gave me the gift
For which I craved above all else
And the chaos mocks me with its
Smug smile at the bringing back
It has given me.

My screams are caught up in my throat
For this is the truth in the nightmare
That is the final good-bye.

Be careful what you wish for, my love,
For while nature and the fates
Seem misaligned,
They do their work nimbly, with efficiency,
And with an ease
That could sweep you away on their next wave.

One plus one is two.
Two plus two is four.
Four plus four is five.

No.

Lost rhythm.

Heat from the slap.
Burns.

One plus one is two.
Two plus two is four.
Four plus four is eight.

Keep the rhythm.

Finish…
So I can.

The warmth of dreaming;
Yet not daring to.

Fantasies pushed back,
Like childhood dreams.

If I tell you that I need to be held
Even though I'm pushing you away
Please don't stop trying to wrap me
In your arms.

If I tell you that I'm struggling
Even though I'm smiling
Please don't believe the face
Because soon the smile will fade.

If I tell you that I'm breaking
Even though I keep getting out of bed
Please tell me that it's ok to hide
Under the covers sometimes.

If I tell you that I'm ok
As my tears cascade
And I try to find a breath
Use your gentle thumbs to caress my skin
And wipe away the pain.

And when the midnight hours threaten to
Smother me
Pull me close
And
Love me until I exist again.

I am confusion;
Not the simplicity
You crave.

The girl grew up with all sorts of romantic ideals brought on by reading those kinds of books and watching those kinds of films. She would spend hours daydreaming about what it would be like to fall hopelessly in love; that kind of love where nothing else in the world mattered.

The boy grew up as something of a rebel; wild and free but always gentle in the small hours of the morning when whispered conversations mean the most.

They grew up at a time where not everyone had mobile phones and living on opposite ends of Ireland was the same as living on different continents. A time where meeting people was either in the local teenage disco, the car park near the swimming pool or in internet chat rooms.

The story isn't so much as boy meets girl, girl likes boy, boy likes girls back, they hold hands, they kiss and allow their 15-year-old minds dream the dreams of their future together. It's more one girl meets boy online, grows tired of boy, another girl talks to boy, gets bored of boy, and finally our girl starts talking to boy... every day.

When girl was finally gifted a mobile phone after months of begging for one, the local payphone suddenly became vacant.

Text

Call

Text

Call

Boy lived at the top of the country; girl lived at the bottom of the country. They were linked only by phone credit and the occasional mailing of a letter; photographs always enclosed.

Girl and boy spoke every day for almost two years and so very much can happen in two years.

They talked about their hopes, their dreams, the good and the bad parts of their days, their families, their friends, their plans for the weekend, who they were both dating; nothing was too much for them to share. They told each other secrets that they daren't share with anybody else.

When girl's first boyfriend broke up with her, boy was on the phone straight away. Once phone credit had gone on both sides, boy sneaked downstairs to use his house phone and girl crept up the hall to use hers.

For 4 hours, he calmed her down, whispered how she deserved more, told her how funny and clever and pretty she was... and told her, for the first time, that he loved her.

Her heart sang... And did not stop singing.

Girl was not allowed to travel by herself to meet boy halfway until she was 17. Boy and girl set the location, set the date, and allowed themselves to get excited. They planned, they decided what they were going to do for their day together, they laughed and looked forward.

The Saturday before boy and girl were due to meet, boy called girl in the middle of the night to ask for her to call him back. With her last few cents of phone credit, she dialled his number. A stolen 30 seconds to talk.

Boy sent girl a text with his last cents.

"Thanks for calling, babes. I will call you tomorrow. I love you. x o x o"

Girl drifted off to sleep with a smile playing on her lips.

Boy did not call girl the next day.

Girl did not worry.

Boy did not call girl the day after.

Girl did not worry.

Boy did not call girl the day after that.

Or after that.

Or after that.

Girl worried.

Girl decided to call boy the day before they were due to meet just to make sure that she should still get on the train; already feeling the shame and embarrassment of travelling to another city, waiting hour after hour and no one coming. Her Cheeks burned with the imagined rejection.

The phone rang once.

The phone rang twice.

"Hello?"

Girl held her breath. It was another girl.

Count to three.

"Hi, I was wondering if I could speak to boy please?"

Muffled sounds.

"Excuse me?"

Girl was sure the other girl was laughing. Girl wanted to smash her phone and sink to the ground.

"Boy died last Sunday. I'm his sister."

Girl did sink to the ground. Girl apologised for the call and said how sorry she was and hung up the phone to boy's number for the last time.

The world spun, life blurred, teenage dreams shattered.

Was it a lie? A really elaborate painful lie?

Girl ran inside and waited for the pain to subside.

There was to be no trip to the city, there was to be no meeting for the first time, there was to be no happily ever after.

Girl googled boy. Boy was dead.

Girl grieved for the first love she never met but does not regret.

To this day, girl still thinks back to boy when times become more complicated than they need to be.

Whispered words after midnight will always make her smile.

Safe
Warm

Tucked in tightly by the promises
That aren't mine to make

My sleep belongs to her soft breath.
Her dreams relax the dark,
A tiny sleeping hand reaching for me,
Pushing aside the nightmares.

From the first moment,
She was all and everything.

Tracing the map that covers my body
Life lines littering my torso
The joys
The tears
The wars
The birth

Learning the story by heart
As my fingers read the braille

Falling in love with my scars
Both seen and unseen

Kiss my wounds
And adore them.
They are not all that I am
But they deserve recognition
As they show a life that has been made
And a life that has been lived

Dreaming and ready
To remember
The taste of you on my tongue

Gin and lust filled

Your breath murmuring whispers of content

I'll settle for the
Moments with your lips
And fall into the edge of the night

I felt like failing
And then what shouldn't
Brought me back

It's you.

But really…

It was me.

Fix your mask

Stand up tall

The   crowd   awaits   your   joke

Once upon a time little girls dreamed of bright futures.

Each night moms and dads would check for monsters under the beds, in the closets, behind the curtains and when they were certain that the coast was clear, gentle kisses of promise would be placed on foreheads, goodnights whispered, and the lights would be turned off.

The little girls would dream of growing up. So many different paths ahead; all leading to happily ever afters.

Unfortunately, as some little girls grow up, the monsters come out from under the bed, evolved into things that moms and dads can't kiss away.

And these monsters will follow the little girls wherever they will go, sowing doubt, wreaking havoc, dashing all hope.

The little girls who had dreamed of Prince Charmings, sunsets and happily ever afters will learn to be careful what they wish for.

Prince Charmings don't always need a yes before they pick you up and carry you away.

Not-so-little girls will learn that what they don't offer can be taken anyway.

They will learn that sometimes Prince Charmings' favourite colours are black and blue and will decorate the not-so-little girls as they please.

The sun will rise but their worlds will grow darker and darker.

Not-so-little girls will feel like there is no way up, no way out. That dreams are just that. Dreams.

They will learn to exist within the shadows and the whispers.

But one day there will be a cry.

One not-so-little girl will crawl out from the night.

Her voice will be small, unsure of what to say and how to say it.

And she will be hushed just as suddenly as she began.

One voice silenced.

She will have been heard though and sparks will have been ignited.

Another voice will pick up her cry. Soon to be joined by another.

And another.
And another.
And another.

Until there are too many voices to be quietened.

They will join together in one melody singing their truths.

And their choruses will echo.

Their song will be heard by all until all can repeat the words by heart.

And the Prince Charmings will know to fear what's coming.

No will mean no.
Stop will mean stop.
No such thing as 'asking for it'.

The blacks and blues will be replaced, repainted with the reds of fiery passion.

The not-so-little girls will grow strong; no longer forced to hide in the shadows.

No longer little girls dreaming of futures with Prince Charmings and the happily ever afters that came with the old storyline.

They will be seen.
They will be heard.
And it will be beautiful.

Women standing tall, cradling the lost little girls within, dreaming now only of the happily ever afters they can carve out for themselves; safe in the knowledge that when they sing their song, the world will listen.

Worthless dirt
Scrub
Scour
Cleanse

Only good for trodding on
Step on
Step firm

I'll try to clean
Wash away
Become something you find pretty
Make you proud

I'll sparkle and I'll shine
I'll please you…

Until you stop playing with me…
And I become encased in
Dust and dirt once again

You'll no longer smile
You'll toss me
And walk away

Dirt has its uses
It gives birth to
Flowers
Trees
Life

Treat me like dirt
If you will
For I see my worth

When the sun shines
I'll think of you
Roses blooming
Bringing back memories
Of childhood summers;
Hugs, laughter, and togetherness.

And when their season is over,
I'll think of untimely goodbyes
And hope that one day
I'll smile for you again.

What did you do for me?

Spread your legs twice.

The child dreams.

Fickle feathers of hope.

Twisted bands of daisy chains
Linking in the light.

Laughter and lawns,
Wishing on dandelions.

The child dreams for the future
With fickle feathers of hope.

The future dreams for the past;
Tears for daisy chains and cut grass.

After midnight
I crave the whispers most.

The promises,
The dreams.

The intimate laughter
That only comes
When secrets are shared and
Shields are shed.

After midnight
Truths are spoken.

Cherish the moments
For dawn will come
All
Too
Soon.

Allowing my body to believe
The white lies of lust
Your lips tell my skin.

Unspoken,
Yet heard.

I'll believe
For after midnight
It suits us both
To pretend to feel
What was never really there.

When the sun comes up
I'll fix my mask
And let you believe
In the beautiful fiction
I've created.

My greatest role, after all,
Has been my life.

I am chasing the dawn
When what I really need
Is sleep.

As the actor forgets their lines
The performance begins to unravel.

Missed entrances, missed steps
Derail the intended story.

The actor persists
Until the last eyes
Have retreated into the night
Taunting perceived failure.

To the empty room,
The actor will take their final bow
And smile
For, at last, the show is over.

At night the little girl cries
Begging for an embrace
To make the monsters go away.

We are bookends.

Connected by beautiful words
But   standing   volumes   of   worlds   apart.

Last night I dreamt that I saw
A dandelion that was ten feet tall.

One head sprouted.
Another grew.
And then the last made for
Three heads in all.

I fixed my body and filled my lungs.
For a beat, I held a breath,
And then blew out with all my might.

The feathery seeds softly flew into the breeze,
Bringing with them my wish to turn back the clock.

The world did not reverse.
It was the same.
Cold and dull,
And filled with pain.

Fighting back any emotion,
I dared myself to try again.

I waited thinking.
I waited hoping.
I waited until the wish was ready

Again, I readied myself to draw a breath.
Steadied myself and stared at the next.

The air was cold as it filled my body.
It stung.
It numbed.

And still I breathed.

I held the breath,
I held it close.
I held it in until it warmed.

Blinking back the tears of fight,
I slightly parted my lips and let go.

Silvery breath flew high and neat,
Slowly, lovingly, separating seed from stem.

And when the stem was bald,
I silently prayed for all.

Still the world did not reverse.

In the stillness, my cheeks grew damp.

As the dark descended, the freeze set in.
The shimmer of the wish declined.

One last wish.

I readied myself and looked to the sky,
Searching for a sign.

Hanging high were 3 great stars,
Twinkling in a line.

"That wish has already been granted", they
whispered.
"You just look everywhere but there."

There?

"But where is there?" I begged.

No answer.

Through the night I pleaded
To no avail.
The resounding unanswered deafened.

As the sun grew strong in the east,
I dragged myself to my feet.
My last wish.
My last ounce of resolve.

I unfurled my crippled body,
I stretched my aching limbs.
I took a breath,
A breath that made me feel;
Feel I could swim to the edge of the bottom of the
ocean.

With a force far beyond my strength,
I let go.

Scattered dreams floated into the dawn
As my wish whispered "Let me find there..."

I want to tell you the good things
As you wrap yourself around me.

Piece me together with your fingertips.

Read between my lines with your lips.

Until the moment comes
When we are whole
And I can't make myself leave your arms
Because I'm ready for another story.

It's loud in small spaces.

Voices clambering to be heard,
Screeching to be the first
To finish their sentence.

Arguments with no winners
And one loser
Who knows it's all a lie.

The fights will continue,
The small space ever more complicated
And the loser makes do with no resolutions.

When your whole life
Is set to rush hour
It's nice to stop
And smell the rain.

Let me love you.

Your histories
And their scars.

Let me hold you
And revel in your voices.

Let me hear your song
And think it beautiful.

Because your stories,
Your scars,
Your songs
Are beautiful.

You wake,
You try,
You fight.

And through it all
Your smile breaks through.

So
Please

Let me love you.

Delicate touches
Full with apprehensive want
Baited breath
Asking if it's alright
To go further
One kiss
Seals the deal
Melting fears
Fixed together
Climbing together
Reaching for release
For just a moment
All that's real is forgotten
Falling for a delicious lie
Because sometimes the
Truth hurts too much

Tasting the tequila
On the tip of your tongue
Fuel to the fire
That already burns
Feeling the heat
I'll savour it
Just
This
Once
More

The silence from
The intended but blank
Birthday card
Speaks volumes.

Last night
I dreamed
You were
My last
Coin.

I bet
You all
On black.

And lost
My mind.

Getting lost in the acres,
Makeshift forts atop the trees,
Pretend ghosts walk the orchard.

The wonder of the rock embedded
In the stream.
At the time it was an island
Sleeping in a vast river
Where we would crouch and camp
And tell our stories.

A childhood spent
Wild and free
And touched
By magic.

There's an empty place at the table
Where Reason should sit.

They're running late.

Apprehensive glances
Full of unsaid dreams.
Holding on tight to the bar
That's closest to your hip.

Let's get off this bus
And go see a film
That's been out to long
To draw a crowd.

And I'll hope that
Our hands will meet
Amongst the popcorn kernels.

Mistakes?

Regret?

If you had not stolen that moment
And fallen down the rabbit hole,
Why, Alice,
You would still be sleep walking your way
With constant wonderings of what might have been.

Are you ok, Mommy?

No, Sweetheart.

I'm worried about
Yesterday and tomorrow
But forgetting about today.

I wipe the corner of your mouth
With the heart on my sleeve
And you look up at me with
Humour and magic
Reminding me of all that I have done right

Playing the games from youth
As attempts are made to climb the ladder.
The same jokes
But with riskier punchlines.
Gone is standing in the corner for bad behaviour,
There's more on the line.
While unseen
The Dunce's hat remains
Serving as a reminder
That power is fleeting
So be mindful of the steps you take.

Scars from the beat
Burns from the bass
Shame from the repeated lyric.

The ghost of an old song
Haunts the hope

If I could breathe
Her dreams into reality
I would breathe
And breathe
Right up to the breath
That finishes my story.

Flying through the air
Racing through the stars
Until the war starts
And all descend
Tumbling to a fate
Unintended for them.

The wings are broken
And it will take
More than wishes
To fix their shattered dreams.

"I am finally that bird.
I am finally free to soar."

Wise words of premonition
That I hold close;
Hold in a way
I should have held
The little girl who wrote them.

I'm late with my embrace
But I'm here now
And I will fight to
Never let her down again.

Fly, little bird.
I will catch you
If you fall.

Watching reflections
Pages flipped to images
Eyes mirroring interest
In subjects further
Than the skins.

Salt and vinegar fingers
Press the button
And a forlorn glance
Is thrown back.

His eyes wish for
A mirrored interest
Of his very own.

He steps off
And out
Forcing joy
Because his belly is full
Even if his heart
Isn't.

The footsteps in the sane
The sparks from fingertip trails
The bubble of laughter from the core
The shared tears of joys and pain.

I am nothing,
We said.
Forgetting the many chapters
We have already completed.

Ignore the bleak, imagined synopsis
That comes from overthinking in the dark;
Colour in your own book cover
Write your own bestseller
Let your heart beat
And your lungs will breathe.

Hold me until I fall asleep
And whisper safe thoughts
To my dreams.

When there is nothing left to say
I find myself still speaking.

Somewhere between 2am and 4am

I fell between

The cracks

I am worth so much more

Than stolen moments in the dark

I am worth the sunrise

I lost myself in you
I left reality at the door
And for a brief time
It didn't matter.

The fears and lies
Did not exist.

I let you fuck me
And you fucked me over.

Read my stories to me
Tell me what you know
And let me hear my magic
As you believe it.

Lay my truths on me
With your lips.

Talk me through my pain
With the caress of your fingertips.

I come alive under your touch
And I breathe through your kiss.

There is magic to be found
During the echoes of the silence of midnight.

Magic lives in the dark;
Help me cast my spells.

The early morning message…

The late-night phone call…

Both are kind.

It's the in-between that bites.

Who knew the Oxford Comma

Could be so sexy…

The silences which once

Seemed so comfortable

Now speak volumes

Craved simplicity

Which grew ever

Complicated with feelings of

"maybe"

A misguided hope

Breaking the walls

That surrounded

The house of cards

Brick by brick

The house falls

For silence was

An omission

And the feelings

Were a lie

I am that secret you keep

The bad habit
No one knows

I am your shame
Hidden behind closed doors
And kept in the shadows

I believed in your whispers

But

You were just hungry
And I was always available

Flashes of names

And faces

And moments

Caught up and lost

In an incoherent storyline.

Dear Being,

I know your stories.

Somewhere betwixt the lies, there are glimpses of a truth that could have been.

One puff.
Two puff.

All hope lost in your smoke.

You come back with your apologies but I am tired of you stealing my forgiveness.

Continue your self-service; and let me start mine.

Regards,
Someone who should have meant more

Paper thin holding paper thin
Taking care of each other as they
Journey up and down the hills.

Their eyes reflect the same stories
From the decades.

Smiling,
Laughing at the same untold joke.

They don't need words because
They
Just
Know.

Look back
Only to see
How far
You have walked.

How close we are to giving up

And yet determined to reach the finish line.

One foot in front of the other

Feeling like the monotonous dance should cease

And yet with a small change

We add our own piece of flavour.

Our proof is in our refusal.

Our strength comes from our battles.

Today is the fight we fight

Making us stronger for the

Unknowns of tomorrow.

Step one:

Breathe.

After Midnight

After Midnight

Printed in Poland
by Amazon Fulfillment
Poland Sp. z o.o., Wrocław

R10058